Pixie Power

by Christine Peymani

PaRragon

Bath · New York · Singapore · Hong Kong · Cologne · Delhi · Melbourne

First published by Parragon in 2007
Parragon
Queen Street House
4 Queen Street
Bath BA1 1HE, UK

ISBN 978-1-4054-8730-6

Printed in China

Chapter 1

"Which brings us to something truly fascinating..." announced Mr Delgado, the chemistry teacher at Stiles High. Sitting at a lab table across from her best friend Cloe, Yasmin hid a gorgeous book on fairies inside her chemistry book. She was mesmerized and too absorbed in it to pay attention to what her teacher was saying. Next to Yasmin, her lab partner, Cymbeline, was struggling to keep her eyes open.

"...zinc," continued the teacher, tapping his pointer against the huge periodic table draped across the front of the room.

As Mr Delgado droned on about zinc, Yasmin gazed at an illustration of a dark fairy transforming into a raven. She was suddenly startled out of her reading by a loud tapping noise at the window beside the lab table she shared with Cloe, Dylan and Cymbeline. Yasmin and Dylan looked up and saw a large, creepy-looking raven peering in at them. Dylan stuck his tongue out at the bird and it flew away.

"All right, let's start your experiments," Mr Delgado said.

Yasmin set her book aside and turned to her lab partners.

"So, where do we start?" she asked.

Cloe and Dylan pulled out their notes, but Cymbeline just stared blankly. Cloe leaned over and shook the girl's shoulder.

"Cymbeline? Hey, Cymbeline!" Cloe called.

Cymbeline woke startled and asked, "Huh? Wha...?"

"Time to do our experiment," Cloe told her.

"Oh," Cymbeline replied with a yawn. "Sorry. Guess I kinda zoned."

Dylan fiddled with a couple of test tubes full of chemicals. "No doubt the little lady was daydreaming – about me," Dylan said, flashing a cheesy smile at his friends.

Suddenly the chemicals erupted, splattering green goo all over Dylan's face.

"Not unless she's into leprechauns," Yasmin replied, laughing at Dylan's stunned expression. She flipped to a leprechaun illustration in her fairy book and showed it to Dylan. "See? They're green like you."

"Very funny," Dylan said, wiping his face.

"Pretty Princess!" Cloe reprimanded. "Reading fairy stories in chemistry class? Bad idea..."

Yasmin's best friends always called her 'Pretty Princess' because of her quiet confidence and regal style. Yasmin was usually such a dedicated student that Cloe was totally surprised at her.

Yasmin looked at Cloe sheepishly. "I know," she admitted. "But it's such a good book!"

Mr Delgado shot them a suspicious look.

"Uh-oh," Cloe whispered. "You're busted."

"Mademoiselle Yasmin? That doesn't look like a chemistry book to me," Mr Delgado said, moving towards their lab table. Yasmin froze, terrified.

A knock on the classroom door distracted Mr Delgado's attention and he turned away from their table. Yasmin heaved a sigh of relief and slipped the book into her bag.

The school principal walked in with a hip and mischievous-looking new girl.

"This is Lina McKnight," he announced. "She's a transfer student."

He handed the girl over and left.

Dylan took in the girl's glossy black hair and cool, neon-accented clothes, and grinned.

"She'll be mine by sixth period," he whispered.

Cloe and Yasmin rolled their eyes.

Cymbeline seemed to perk up at the sight of the new girl. Lina shot Cymbeline a cool, authoritative look, and then headed for an empty seat near the back of the room.

Dylan pulled a little black book from his rucksack and flipped it open.

"Lina," he said. "I've just gotta get her number for my LBB."

"Your what?" Yasmin asked.

"LBB." The girls looked at him blankly, and Dylan continued. "You know – 'little black book'. I've got all my honeys in there."

"Oh yeah?" Cloe grabbed it from him and sifted through the pages while Dylan tried to take it back.

"Hey, that's mine!" he protested.

"Dylan, you haven't gone out with any of the girls in this book," Cloe declared.

Dylan just shrugged and then turned to stare at Lina.

"Okay, back to work!" Mr Delgado ordered the class.

"C'mon, guys," Cloe said, taking out a sheet of paper. "Did everyone do their equations?"

Dylan held up his answer sheet. "Yep!"

"Right here," Yasmin added, pulling a piece of paper out of her bag.

Cymbeline looked at her lab partners apologetically. "Sorry. I forgot."

"Cymbeline! I've got to get an A in this class!" Cloe cried.

The others turned to Cymbeline, waiting for an explanation.

"Oh come on, it's just one assignment," Cymbeline scoffed. "You act like it's some kind of disaster."

Cloe and Yasmin exchanged worried looks.

Dylan, in the meantime, was swirling some chemicals in a beaker. He held the mixture out towards Lina and asked, "Hey! Got chemistry?"

Lina shook her head and flipped her long black hair over her shoulder. Dylan looked disappointed.

The bell rang and students started filing out of the room. Dylan slung his rucksack over his shoulder, wiping the last globs of green from his face, and trailed after Lina.

From another classroom, a cute younger girl appeared in Dylan's path, "Hi Dylan!" she said cheerfully.

Dylan crashed into the girl, his eyes still fixed on Lina. The younger girl's books flew everywhere, and Dylan absentmindedly helped her pick them up as he watched Lina strut away. "Oh, uh, sorry, uh..." Dylan stammered. He looked at the girl as though he couldn't quite remember who she was.

"It's Breeana," she reminded him. "Cymbeline's little sister?"

"Oh, right, yeah," Dylan replied, distracted.

"Hey, I was wondering..." Breanna began. She looked down nervously at her armful of books, then forced herself to continue, "...are you going to the Magnolia Ball?" The words came out in a rush and then she just stood there, staring hopefully at Dylan.

Lina stopped to get a drink at a nearby water fountain, and when she turned around, she noticed Breeana talking to Dylan. She sashayed towards them, a haughty smile on her lips.

Dylan noticed Lina coming towards him, "Yup, that's right. She's finally feeling the chemistry," he said foolishly to himself.

"What?" Breeana asked, confused.

"Her radar is picking up my love waves," Dylan continued.

"Excuse me?" She turned to see what Dylan was staring at, and saw Lina smiling at them. She turned back to Dylan and took in his lovesick gaze.

"Oh," she said, looking hurt.

Lina winked at Dylan, then strode away.

"Oh, I'm sorry," Dylan said, remembering where he was. "Did you ask me something?

"No," Breeana said sadly. "Nothing. Never mind." She walked away, her shoulders slumped with disappointment.

Cloe, Yasmin and Cymbeline emerged from their classroom. "See, Cloe?" Cymbeline said. "What were you so stressed about? We finished."

"No thanks to you and your little siesta," Cloe accused.

"Whatever," Cymbeline snapped. She started to take off down the hall, but Yasmin blocked her path.

"Hey, Cymbeline, wait a sec," Yasmin said, pulling the girl off to the side. "You know, sometimes I have to bring a book to class to keep chemistry interesting," she admitted, "but if you don't get with it soon, you're gonna fail."

"Ugh. I just sat through one lecture," Cymbeline sighed, "please, spare me another one."

"What's going on?" Yasmin demanded. "Lately you seem...different."

"Well I guess some people grow up," Cymbeline replied. "Others...don't. Gotta fly."

Cloe and Yasmin were flabbergasted by Cymbeline's snide remark. The two friends watched, stunned, as Cymbeline flitted away. She approached Lina, who was standing alone, and whispered something to her. Both girls glanced back at Cloe and Yasmin and sniggered before walking away.

Dylan joined his friends and asked, "Does Cymbeline know her?"

"How could she?" Cloe asked. "Lina's new."

"I don't know, but there's something strange going on with those two," Yasmin replied.

Dylan stroked his chin thoughtfully. "You know

what that Lina girl needs? A date for the Magnolia Ball, and I know just the guy!"

Sasha and Jade joined their best friends in the hallway.

"Hey, " Sasha said.

"Hi," Yasmin replied, still distracted by her confrontation with Cymbeline.

"You know," Cloe told Dylan, "maybe if you kept your focus on just one girl, that girl might finally take you seriously."

"You don't understand," Dylan protested. "I consider it my duty to share the wealth of irresistible cool that is the Dyl-meister—"

He was interrupted by the loud cawing of the raven they'd seen earlier. It swept down on Dylan, making him shriek as he tried to wave it away. The raven grabbed his rucksack in its beak and flew off through an open window.

"Whoa! Did you see that?" Yasmin exclaimed.

"Hey!" Dylan cried, "my comb's in there! And my hair gel!" A look of horror spread across his face. "And my LBB! Come back here, you mangy bird!"

He ran out of the door, chasing the raven.

"There goes Mr Irresistibly Cool," Sasha said with a laugh.

Chapter 2

Outside, Dylan hopped on his motorcycle and raced down the country road heading away from Stilesville. He desperately followed the raven flying ahead of him, his rucksack dangling from its talons.

"Hey, my love life's in there!" Dylan shouted, shaking his fist at the bird. But the raven just cawed back at him, then flew into the woods that bordered the road.

"Oh no, not off-roading," Dylan complained. "I hate off-roading! I mean, come on, this isn't a dirt bike." But there was no way he was letting that bird have his rucksack, so he turned and drove into the woods, his motor revving choppily as brush crackled beneath his tyres.

"Agh! Ugh! Oof!" Dylan cried as he fought to navigate through the forest, dodging low-hanging branches and rocks in his path.

He burst into a misty clearing strewn with leaves, mushrooms and mossy fallen trees. His motorcycle hit a log and he flipped over, landing on the ground with a thud. He picked himself up, bruised but otherwise fine, and yanked off his helmet.

"Where are you, huh?" he demanded. "Come out here, you stupid bird!"

An owl hooted from somewhere among the trees, its call echoing hollowly through the clearing. A spooky-sounding bird shrieked back threateningly.

Dylan gulped, frightened. "You know, on second thoughts, why don't you keep the rucksack? None of those girls called me back, anyway!"

He turned towards his motorcycle and jumped back, startled. He had left his bike on the ground where it had fallen, but now it sat upright – and leaning against it was Lina.

"Lina! Wh-where'd you come from?" Dylan stammered, totally spooked.

"Missing something?" Lina asked casually, holding up Dylan's rucksack.

©MGA

"My rucksack!" Dylan exclaimed. "How'd you get it back?"

Lina stepped forward, staring into his eyes, "We wouldn't want you to lose your LBB, now would we?" she teased.

Dylan backed away nervously. "Uh...right. I mean, how'd you-? Well, uh, I gotta get going. I'm late for my cooking class."

Lina reached out and grabbed his hand, smiling mischievously. "C'mere. There's something I wanna show you."

"I-I've kinda gotta get back," Dylan insisted. "See, we're m-moving on from toast and-"

"You're not afraid of a little adventure, are you?" Lina asked.

"N-no. Of course not!" Dylan protested. "I follow strange girls into the forest all the time!"

"That's what I thought," Lina replied. "Come on, follow me. We're going somewhere way cooler than cooking class. Can you hear it?"

Dylan heard a far-off sound, a techno dance music beat. "Hey..." he said, a confused smile spreading across his face.

"Sounds good, right?" Lina asked.

"Yeah," Dylan replied. "But where's it coming from?"

"I'll be only too happy to show you," Lina said with a sly smile.

Still holding his hand, Lina led Dylan to the other side of the clearing. She stopped at a huge, dead tree with a large, cave-like opening beneath it. The music seemed to be coming from inside. Dylan followed Lina towards it, completely mesmerized.

Outside the Stilesville mall, Cloe and Yasmin were hanging a banner announcing "Magnolia Ball — This Saturday!" across the branches of a huge, gorgeous magnolia tree. White petals from the tree's beautiful flowers fluttered down around the girls as they draped strands of white light among the branches.

"And...done!" Cloe said, taking a step back to admire their work.

"Great job, Angel," Yasmin declared. Cloe was known as 'Angel' to her friends because of her high-flying imagination and heavenly style.

Sasha and Jade strolled up to join them.

"Hey, ladies," Sasha said. "I just met with the DJ, and let me tell you, the music is gonna be jammin'!"

"That's great, Bunny Boo," Cloe replied. The girls all called Sasha 'Bunny Boo' because she was totally down with the hip-hop scene.

"The caterer's all set, too," Jade added.

"Awesome, Kool Kat," Yasmin said. Jade's nickname was 'Kool Kat' because she was always on the cutting edge of the latest trends.

"Where's Cymbeline?" Sasha asked. "I thought she was meeting you here."

"Yeah, well, she flaked," Cloe replied.

"But her dad's funding the ball!" Sasha protested. "And she's in charge of organizing it! She wouldn't just flake."

"Something must've come up," Jade added. "That's not like her."

"I don't know what's like her any more," Yasmin said.

Jade and Sasha looked at their friends questioningly, and Cloe explained, "We think she's in some kind of trouble."

"What?" Sasha cried. "No way. Not Cymbeline. She's the most together person I know."

"Not any more," Yasmin insisted.

"Something's up and I want to know what it is," Cloe declared. "You know what? I think we should go over to her house right now and find out."

"Bad idea," Jade interrupted. "You know how strict her dad is — no one's ever been invited to the Devlin home. You'd better just call her."

"We tried!" Yasmin replied. "But she's not picking up her mobile. Look, Cloe's right. I think this is serious."

"Okay, if you say so," Sasha agreed reluctantly.

"What about you?" Yasmin asked.

"Sure," Jade said. "I'm always up for helping a friend in need."

The wind blew and the magnolia tree showered the girls with its huge white flowers.

"Pretty!" Cloe exclaimed in delight.

The girls packed up their things and headed for the Devlin house.

Chapter 3

That night, Cymbeline sneaked through her living room, all decked out in hipster party gear. As she headed for the door, Breeana popped out of the shadows and asked, "Taking off?"

Cymbeline jumped back and gasped, "Breeana! What are you doing sneaking around?"

"I'm not the one sneaking around," Breeana replied. "So, where are you going, all dressed up like that?"

"None of your business," Cymbeline snapped.

"Since when is it none of my business?" her sister asked, hurt. "We tell each other everything."

"Says who?" Cymbeline demanded.

"Fine," Breanna replied, heading for the stairs. "I'll just ask Dad where you're going. I'm sure you've got permission to go out."

Cymbeline's eyes widened in alarm. She grabbed Breeana by the wrist and snarled, "You do that, and you can forget you ever had a sister!"

"Ow!" Breeana cried. "You're hurting me."

Cymbeline relaxed her grip and said sweetly, "I'm sorry. It's just...it's a secret, okay? I don't want Dad to know. We've always kept each other's secrets, haven't we?"

"But..." Breeana paused, unsure of what to say, but then an idea struck her. "Why can't I come with you?"

Cymbeline hesitated, and then gave her sister a big smile. "Maybe...if you promise not to tell Dad. Where I'm going is really great – I can't wait to show you!"

"Really?" Breeana asked,

©MGA

intrigued. "What is it?"

Just then, their intercom buzzed. Cloe, Sasha, Jade and Yasmin stood outside the gate of the Devlin home beside an intercom. A big stone wall lined the pavement, completely blocking their view of the house.

"See?" Jade said, gesturing to the wall. "I told you they like their privacy."

"No one's home," Sasha declared. "Let's go."

"Yeah," Jade agreed. "I have to finish my essay on the History of Modern Law Enforcement."

As they turned to leave, a voice came out of the intercom. "Hello?" It was Breeana.

Yasmin leaned toward the intercom and said, "Hey, Breeana, it's Yasmin. And Sasha and Jade and Cloe. Is Cymbeline home?"

Inside, Cymbeline narrowed her eyes at the intercom box. "I'm not here," she hissed. "Get rid of them."

Breeana looked at her sister imploringly, then turned back to the intercom and replied, "No. She's not here."

"Can we come in and talk to you?" Yasmin asked.

"Talk to me?" Breeana asked, surprised.

"About Cymbeline," Cloe added.

"Wh-what about Cymbeline?" Breeana asked nervously.

"Why don't you let us in?" Sasha suggested. "We'll explain inside."

"Uh...sorry, I can't. My dad said no guests till I finish my homework," Breeana explained.

"Well, let us in and we'll talk to him, then," Cloe insisted.

"Geez, Cloe!" Jade whispered. "Do you have to be so pushy?"

"No!" Breeana shouted. Then, lowering her voice again, she continued, "I mean, he's not here either.

Gotta go. Homework. Bye." The speaker clicked off.

Cloe and Yasmin turned to each other. "Yas, did we drive all the way out here to take 'no' for an answer?" Cloe asked.

"I think not," Yasmin replied. "Give me a boost."

"Whoa — wait a minute!" Jade protested. "That's trespassing!"

"So?" Yasmin asked. "We're just helping a friend in need."

"What if she's a friend in need of some privacy?" Sasha asked.

"Let's just wait till we see her at school," Jade suggested.

"But I have a bad feeling..." Cloe insisted.

"Drama-Mama, you've had a lot of bad feelings that turn out to be nothing," Sasha replied. Cloe was the most dramatic of the girls, and frequently got carried away with her wild hunches and ideas.

"But sometimes they're right!" Cloe cried.

"Yeah, but I'm not breaking and entering based on 'a bad feeling'," Jade replied.

"We just want to help," Yasmin said.

"Look, I'm just not into poking my nose into other people's business," Sasha declared.

"Fine," Yasmin snapped. "You don't have to come. But can you at least wait for us and give us a ride home?"

"That's aiding and abetting," Jade pointed out. Yasmin and Cloe glared at their friend.

"All right, all right, we'll wait," Sasha sighed. She helped Cloe boost Yasmin over the wall.

"Doesn't anyone care about my bad feeling?" Jade asked. "The one where I feel like we're gonna end up in jail?"

Yasmin ignored her, scrambling over the wall and stepping on Cloe's head in the process.

"Ow!" Cloe cried.

Yasmin reached the top of the wall and peered down over the other side. "Now the question is, how do I get— waaahhh!"

She slipped, tumbled off the wall and crashed into a pile of branches with a thud.

"Are you okay?" Jade called.

There was no answer but, a moment later, the gate swung open to reveal Yasmin with twigs in her hair and a dishevelled outfit.

"No probs," Yasmin said. "Come on in."

Cloe headed through the gate, then turned to see Jade and Sasha backing away.

"You're on your own," Sasha announced.

"Hey, I thought we always stuck together!" Cloe complained.

"Yeah, we'll stick together back at the car," Jade replied.

"Fine," Cloe said in a huff. She turned on her heel and closed the gate behind her, leaving Jade and Sasha outside.

Cloe and Yasmin headed down the stone walkway, looking around in amazement. The walkway led through a flowing, tree-covered garden to a gorgeous modern-style wooden house. The property overlooked the gorgeous, twinkling lights of Stilesville, spread out across the valley below.

"Wow, look at this place!" Cloe exclaimed.

"It's beautiful!" Yasmin agreed.

"When I'm out of school, I'm building a house just like this one..." Cloe said, as she tripped over a garden gnome and ended up sprawled out on the grass, "...except for the deadly garden gnome in the middle of the walkway!" She picked up the gnome and put it beside the path.

They headed for the front door, and Yasmin rang the doorbell. They waited, but no one answered. They were about to give up when they heard soft voices coming from the greenhouse alongside the house.

The girls exchanged looks, and then headed down the curved pathway towards the greenhouse, past the stables. A horse whinnied, breaking the silence and making both girls jump.

"That totally scared me!" Cloe cried.

"I didn't know they had horses," Yasmin added.

When they reached the greenhouse, they could see the silhouette of a large man, who they assumed was Mr Devlin, through the steamy glass windows. They couldn't see who he was talking to, but it looked like something was fluttering near his head. They heard a high-pitched voice say, "But Sire, a forgotten evil one has returned — an evil that is no stranger to you."

Cloe and Yasmin looked at each other, confused. This wasn't like any other conversation they'd ever heard!

"Darkness creeps back into the forest," the voice continued. "The freelands and their good people will be in peril."

"Did you hear that?" Cloe whispered. Yasmin nodded excitedly. The Devlin household was way more mysterious than they'd thought!

As the girls crept around the corner, Cloe tripped again. She looked down and saw the same gnome lying in front of her.

"What the-?" Cloe asked, looking from the garden gnome to the walkway where she'd tripped on it before, all the way across the garden. "Wasn't that-?"

The gnome grinned up at her with its blank, ceramic smile.

Cloe and Yasmin heard movement in the greenhouse and quickly hid behind a bush. Mr Devlin stuck his head out the door and peered around. He looked a lot smaller outside than he had through the window. When he didn't see

30

©MGA

anything, he headed back inside.

The girls heaved a sigh of relief, and were starting to get up when a pair of hands grabbed them by the shoulders. They turned to find Breeana standing behind them, looking panicked.

"My dad cannot know that you two are here," she whispered. She steered them away from the greenhouse.

"Well, we are here," Cloe replied.

"And we're not leaving until you tell us what's going on with Cymbeline," Yasmin added.

Breeana led them towards the front gate, not answering.

Cloe stopped in her tracks. "So are you gonna tell us, or do we have to ask your dad?"

"Shhh," Breeana whispered. "Come on, you wouldn't do that..."

"Try us," Cloe said.

"There's nothing going on," Breeana insisted.

The girls heard a door open back at the house.

"Aha!" Yasmin cried. "She is here, isn't she?"

"No, of course not," Breeana answered innocently. Cloe strode towards the house with Yasmin following behind her and Breeana chasing after them.

"We'll see about that," Cloe declared.

"Please, stop! Don't go up there," Breeana begged.

Cloe and Yasmin noticed some sparkling lights behind the house and headed over to them. A techno beat wafted out towards them. Then a crimson pinpoint streaked in from the distance and hovered above Stilesville.

"What's that?" Yasmin asked. "I think something's on fire."

Breeana tried to pull Cloe away, but Cloe broke free of the younger girl's grasp. She and Yasmin hurried around the side of the house and saw Cymbeline standing on a little hill, concentrating. Suddenly, in a shower of incandescent droplets, a pair of neon wings burst forth from her back. Cymbeline fluttered her wings, shaking off more light droplets, then beat them swiftly and rocketed into the sky in a streak of white light. Soon she was nothing more than a bright white pinpoint. She joined the scarlet light over the valley, and then they both streaked away, the music fading with them.

Cloe and Yasmin watched all of this, stunned. "What? Who? How?" Cloe sputtered, turning to Breeana. Then she shrieked, "Ow! Something bit me!"

"You know, I think it's time you nosy girls got yourselves a million miles away from here," said a voice with a thick Irish accent.

"Ow! Someone kicked me!" Yasmin yelped.

That was enough for Cloe. "Run!" she shouted. Breeana watched helplessly as the girls fled towards the gate. Over their shoulders, they saw a tiny man who looked like the garden gnome tearing after them, hurling wads of grass and mud at their backs.

"You should know when you're not wanted," he ranted. "Go on, get outta here! Skedaddle! A fine day it is when a pair of non-fairy folks go traipsin' about the premises like they own the place!"

"Faster!" Yasmin urged. "He's right behind us!"

"Oh, if His Majesty knew of it... he'd banish me down by the carp pond with the pixies, frogs and snakes," the little man wailed. "Demoted and doomed for all eternity, I'd be!"

The girls reached the gate and it magically opened for them. They dashed through and it slammed shut behind them.

Chapter 4

At Stiles High the next day, Lina stood leaning over the railing at the top of the stairs. She spotted Dylan walking through the lobby below.

"Oh, loverboy!" she called.

Dylan spotted Lina and skipped up to the stairway landing.

"Yes, Lina, my master," he said, his voice overly enthusiastic. "M-A-S-T-E-R. Master," he spelled. "What can I do for you? Name anything. A-N-Y-T-"

A group of students approached and Lina clamped her hand over Dylan's mouth. "Stop it, stop it, STOP IT," she hissed. "Try to remember. You're my servant because you're under a spell — you're not a servant who spells!"

"I'm sorry! S-O-R-R-" Dylan began, but Lina held up a hand to stop him.

"One more letter and you're fairy dust!" she growled threateningly.

"Sorry," Dylan replied, hanging his head.

"Do you remember your instructions?" Lina demanded.

"Do I ever!" Dylan exclaimed, perking up.

"I'm counting on you," Lina threatened. "Now go!"

"I am your humble servant," Dylan said softly. Then he hopped onto the banister and slid down it, gleefully shouting, "Wheeee!"

Sasha and Jade were standing at their lockers busily putting away books while Cloe and Yasmin tried to explain what had happened the night before.

"And then a weird little man came out of nowhere, totally freaked out and chased us off the property!" Cloe finished.

Sasha whirled around, looking annoyed. "Why don't you give it a rest, Cloe?" she demanded. "April Fool's Day was two weeks ago – I think you're a little late."

"I swear it's true," Cloe insisted. Sasha looked at her sceptically and Cloe added, "I swear it on – on my new boots!"

Jade checked out Cloe's boots, "Those are totally stylin'."

Cloe turned her leg to show off the boots from different angles. "Thanks!" she replied. "I got 'em on sale."

"Nice," Jade said, "but I still don't believe you."

"Look, we both saw Cymbeline fly off in a flash of white light! And then that crazy little man chased us off the garden," Yasmin insisted.

"He kinda looked like a gnome...a really angry little

gnome," Cloe explained. She turned to Yasmin, an idea hitting her. "In fact, he looked just like that garden gnome I kept tripping over!"

"That's true!" Yasmin agreed, but Sasha and Jade just looked at them in exasperation. They slammed their lockers shut simultaneously and turned to leave.

"Wait!" Yasmin pleaded, grabbing Jade's sleeve. "What about Cymbeline? I mean, we saw the girl sprout wings."

"Yas, you've gotta stop reading those fairy stories you've been into lately," Jade said, pulling away from her friend's grip. "They're starting to fry your brain."

"I just think you both need more sleep," Sasha added. She headed down the hallway, shaking her head. "You're having, like, a shared hallucination!"

Dylan sauntered up to the girls, a goofy grin plastered across his face as he sang, "Mares eat oats, and does eat oats and little lambs eat ivy. A kid'll eat ivy too, wouldn't you?" He gave a little bow and exclaimed, "Greetings, mi'ladies!"

"Your what?" Sasha asked, staring at him. "What's your deal now?"

"Seriously?" Jade chimed in. "You were supposed to help me hang lights for the ball yesterday, and you never showed up."

"Oh, I've been here, there and everywhere," Dylan replied cheerfully. "Hither and yon, you know. And now I must take my leave. I'm late, I'm late, for a very important date!" He gave them a little wave and did a quick twirl, then called, "Toodles for now!" as he pranced off down the hallway.

"What's got into him?" Yasmin asked.

"I don't know, but he sure seems happy," Sasha said.

"Really happy," Jade agreed.

"Bizarrely happy," Cloe added.

"Suspiciously happy," Yasmin finished.

"Well, we can worry about that later," Sasha said. "Now we've just gotta get to class. We'll see you after school, right? There's a ton of decorating left to do!"

"Sure," Yasmin replied. Sasha and Jade strolled off together, leaving Cloe and Yasmin alone.

"They don't believe us!" Cloe cried, slumping against her locker.

"Of course they don't," Yasmin said. "I wouldn't believe us, either."

©MGA

Cloe spotted Breeana and grabbed Yasmin's arm, dragging her down the hall.

"There's Breeana," she exclaimed. "If anyone can help prove our story, it's her!"

Breeana sulked down the hallway, anxiously looking from side to side. She turned to peer over her shoulder and nearly smacked into Cloe and Yasmin.

"Oh...hi!" Breeana gasped.

"We've been looking all over for you," Yasmin said.

"Huh," Breeana replied. "Really?"

"What in the world is going on?" Cloe demanded.

"Wh-what makes you think something's going on?" Breeana asked.

"Well, your sister can fly, for one thing," Cloe said. "That was sort of the red flag."

"Shhh!" Breeana hissed, her eyes darting around nervously.

"Well? Are you gonna explain last night to us, or not?" Yasmin asked quietly.

"I-I can't," Breeana told them. "I have to be somewhere right now."

"Uh-uh," Cloe replied, blocking the younger girl's path. "You aren't going anywhere till you tell us what really happened last night."

"No," Breeana said. "No, I have to go right now."

"Then we'll come with you," Cloe suggested. "You can explain on the way."

But Breeana shook her head. "I have to go alone," she insisted.

"Why? Where are you going?" Yasmin asked.

"Uh...I'm meeting someone. It's personal." Breeana backed away, ready to bolt.

"What, like a date or something?" Cloe asked.

A dreamy grin spread across Breeana's face. "Kinda," she said coyly. "Yeah...I guess you could call it a date. So I can't just bring friends along, okay?"

"So who's this hot date with, anyway?" Yasmin asked.

Breeana looked from Yasmin to Cloe uncertainly.

"C'mon, 'fess up!" Cloe insisted. "Who's the lucky guy? Anyone we know?"

"Yeah," Breeana admitted.

"Really? Who is it?" Yasmin demanded.

"Dylan," Breeana whispered shyly.

"Dylan!" Yasmin and Cloe exclaimed.

"Shhh!" Breeana cried. "Yeah, Dylan asked me to meet him somewhere after school."

"Where?" Cloe asked.

"Widow's Hollow," Breeana told them.

"Are you kidding?" Yasmin demanded.

"Look, I-I gotta go," Breeana replied.

"But why would Dylan want you to meet him all the way out there?" Yasmin asked. "I mean, Dylan doesn't even like the woods."

"Well, that's where he said to meet him," Breeana insisted. "Look, I've been hoping he'd ask me to the Magnolia Ball — so maybe he just wanted to pick a really romantic spot to do it."

"There's nothing romantic about Widow's Hollow," Cloe replied. "It's totally creepy."

"Yeah, there's something weird going on here," Yasmin agreed.

"We're going with you," Cloe announced.

"No-" Breeana protested, but when she saw the determined looks on Cloe and Yasmin's faces, she knew there was no point in arguing. "Okay," she agreed reluctantly.

Chapter 5

When Cloe, Yasmin and Breeana reached the woods, a thick fog hung over them, making it almost impossible to see. Walking side by side, the three girls crept cautiously toward Widow's Hollow.

"Ow!" Yasmin cried, colliding with a bush. "Thorns!"

"I know! They scratched up my new boots!" Cloe wailed. "They're completely ruined."

"You don't have to come with me, you know," Breeana said.

"Yes we do," Yasmin replied. She stopped, and the other two stopped behind her. She put her hands on Breeana's shoulders, looked her straight in the eye, and said seriously, "Look, it's just not a good idea to agree to meet a guy alone in the woods. I mean, Dylan's harmless, but still. What were you thinking?"

"She's a freshman," Cloe said. "She doesn't know any better."

Breeana looked like she was about to cry, but a weird, high-pitched sound of singing in the distance interrupted her.

"Shhh," she said. "Do you hear that?"

The fog was so thick that she had no idea where the sound was coming from.

©MGA

"Sure the girls from Killarney, they fill you with blarney,
the talk of their beauty would drive you insane;
and the girls from the city,
though they drink themselves pretty,
could never compare with the girls of Coleraine."

"It sounds like an Irish folk tune," Yasmin whispered.

"But why would someone be singing it in the forest?" Cloe wondered. The girls crept forward, following the sound until it seemed to be right in front of them.

They carefully parted the branches to reveal Dylan skipping around the edge of a clearing. He paused every few seconds to pick a lily or a daisy and add it to the crown of flowers on his head.

"Whoa," Cloe murmured. She and Yasmin stared at their friend, totally stunned.

Breeana tried to push past them. "There's

Dylan!" she exclaimed. Cloe and Yasmin grabbed her and pulled her back.

"Wait," Yasmin whispered.

"Something's wrong with Dylan," Cloe added. "This is not like him at all." Her eyes widened and she asked, "Do you think he has rabies?"

"Anything's possible," Yasmin replied. "Especially after what we saw last night." Turning to Breeana, she said, "You stay here. We'd better talk to him first."

"Okay," Breeana agreed reluctantly.

Cloe and Yasmin approached Dylan, who was now dancing a crazed jig. He jumped and twirled and spun until he was face to face with his friends.

"Since when are you Lord of the Dance?" Cloe asked him.

Dylan just smiled, holding out a lily to each of the girls. "For you, my treasures," he said.

"Dylan, did you get into Mr Delgado's chemistry

supplies? Was there some sort of accident?" Yasmin asked.

Dylan gave a loud, hooting laugh. Without answering, he tossed the lilies into the air and skipped away. He headed deeper into the woods, whistling his Irish tune as he went.

"Hey, get back here!" Yasmin called, but Dylan had already disappeared between the trees. The girls followed the sound of his whistling, but suddenly the woods got much darker, and there was still no sign of Dylan.

"Where'd he go?" Cloe asked nervously. The woods had grown very dark, and the girls clutched each other's hands as they moved forward. Glowing eyes began to appear around them in the darkness, until they were surrounded.

Cloe and Yasmin huddled together, terrified. Then Lina stepped forward and demanded, "What are you doing here?" Looking behind her, she called, "Dylan! You've been very naughty. I told you to bring Breeana, not these girls!"

Behind a cluster of bushes nearby, Breeana watched in horror.

"Whoopsie! My bad," she heard Dylan reply from somewhere in the woods.

"Look who's crashed our party," Lina said. At her voice, the eyes moved forward, and Cloe and Yasmin saw that they were actually glowing spots on the wings of hundreds of dark fairies, just like the one Yasmin had seen in her fairy book.

The fairies giggled cruelly as they stepped towards the girls. Piles of leaves began to whirl around Cloe and Yasmin as the fairies' laughter became a haunting, whispery sound. Then Lina held up her hand and the laughter suddenly stopped.

"And of course, let's not forget our guest of honour," Lina announced. She gestured dramatically and called, "Come along, Princess."

Cymbeline stepped out of the darkness, looking

exhausted. She smirked at Cloe and Yasmin.

"Hey girls," she said.

"Cymbeline?" Yasmin asked.

"What are you doing here?" Cloe added.

In the bushes behind them, Breeana clapped her hand over her mouth, shocked by the sight of her sister.

Yasmin stepped toward Lina and demanded, "What's going on here?"

"Oh, you'll find out," Lina replied with a laugh. "Believe me, you'll find out."

The dark fairies responded with a chorus of mean-spirited laughter.

Cloe and Yasmin looked at each other fearfully. They gave each other a nod and tried to make a run for it, but suddenly vines snaked around their legs and lifted them off the ground, leaving them dangling upside down from the trees.

Dylan popped out right in front of their faces

and exclaimed, "Now we can all dance together! Hooray!" He frolicked off, dancing around the dark fairies, who sniggered at his antics.

Back in her hiding place, Breeana shifted slightly, and a branch snapped beneath her feet. She gasped at the sound, and Lina whirled towards her.

"What was that?" Lina demanded.

Breeana backed silently out of the bushes and sneaked away through the woods, feeling panic but forcing herself to move slowly. Lina peered into the darkness suspiciously, but when she heard nothing else, she turned back to her prisoners, the cruel grin back on her face.

Chapter 6

Sasha and Jade strode through the Stilesville mall, their arms full of rolled-up posters for the Magnolia Ball, streamers, balloons and tons of other decorations. They had already hung posters all over the mall, and now were heading for the doors.

"I can't believe Cloe and Yasmin didn't show," Sasha said. "Do you think they were that mad at us for not believing their crazy story?"

"That's no excuse," Jade replied. "Friends are supposed to stick together, no matter what. This really isn't like them."

Sasha glanced up and gasped. "Jade! Look!"

She pointed down the hallway, where Cloe and Yasmin were approaching, decked out in stylized fairy costumes. Cymbeline and Lina strolled beside them, while Dylan traipsed along behind, carrying their shopping bags. Sasha and Jade walked right up to their friends.

"Hey guys," Sasha said accusingly. "What's the big idea?"

Cloe and Yasmin stared at their best friends blankly.

"I'm sorry, were you speaking to me?" Yasmin asked, her voice flat.

"Why haven't you guys called us back?" Jade demanded. "And why didn't you show up for the Ball Committee meeting?"

"Uh, I dunno...I guess we just found something more interesting to do, than like, saving a tree," Cloe said snidely.

Sasha and Jade exchanged shocked looks.

"Okay, what's going on

here?" Sasha demanded.

"I don't know what you mean," Yasmin replied.

"Well, for one thing, why are you dressed like that?" Jade asked, gesturing to their neon-accented outfits and fake fairy wings.

"Like it?" Cloe did a little twirl to show off her outfit. "We're going to a costume party tonight."

"Um, excuse me, but tonight is the Magnolia Ball," Sasha said. "Since we planned it, I think we kind of need to be there."

"Whatever," Yasmin said with a shrug. "Sounds like a drag. I'd let you come to the party with us, but...well...you're not invited."

"But we're all supposed to be at the Magnolia Ball at nine!" Jade wailed. "Don't you remember?"

"Too bad — our party starts at nine," Cloe replied.

"So you're really going to miss the ball?" Sasha cried.

"You girls are kind of slow, aren't you?"

Lina asked, looking from Jade to Sasha with a wicked smile on her face.

Cymbeline cackled. "They sure are!"

"But Cymbeline, you're the head of the committee," Sasha said. "Your father is funding the ball. I can't believe you would just bail."

"Well, believe it," Cymbeline snapped.

"Come along, ladies," Lina called.

Cymbeline, Yasmin and Cloe immediately turned on their heels and followed Lina down the hall. But then Lina paused and turned back to Sasha and Jade.

"By the way, you don't happen to know where Breeana is, do you?" she asked.

"Breeana?" Sasha asked. "No."

"We, like, really need to know where she went," Cymbeline chimed in.

"Oh yeah?" Jade demanded. "Well, I, like, really need to know where my friends Yasmin and Cloe went. Have you seen them?"

Yasmin, Cloe, Cymbeline and Lina doubled over with laughter, then straightened and flitted away.

Dylan did a few complicated high-stepping dance moves for Sasha and Jade and then leaned in to ask, "Fancy a dance?"

Sasha and Jade glared at him.

"Well then, mustn't dilly-dally!" Dylan exclaimed. "Duty calls."

He pranced off after Lina. Sasha and Jade watched him go, horrified at what had happened to their friends.

©MGA

Outside, Sasha and Jade approached the magnolia tree. The whole area was decorated for the dance, with tables and chairs set up around a dance floor beneath the tree's sweeping branches. It looked gorgeous, but Sasha and Jade didn't even notice.

They headed towards a nearby table to drop off their supplies, but Sasha tripped on her way over, "Whoa!" she yelped, decorations flying everywhere.

"Sasha, what happened?" Jade asked, rushing to her friend's side.

"I–I don't know," Sasha replied. She looked down and saw a garden gnome lying beside her. "Ow. Who put that creepy garden gnome there?"

Jade helped Sasha up and together they gathered up the scattered supplies.

"What is up with our two best friends?" Jade fretted as they worked. The usually calm and collected Kool Kat sounded ready to cry.

"I think that new girl did something to them," Sasha replied. Suddenly she heard what sounded like sobs coming from behind the magnolia tree. "What's that?" she asked, leading Jade towards the sound.

They walked around the tree's huge trunk and there, huddled on the ground, sobbing softly, was Breeana.

"Breeana, what's wrong?" Jade asked.

"I...I..." Breeana began, but she was crying too hard to finish.

"Your sister's looking for you," Sasha told her.

Breeana immediately sprang up from the ground in terror. "Where is she?" she demanded.

"She took off," Jade replied. Breeana looked relieved, and Jade asked, "Wait, are you, like, hiding from her?"

Breeana nodded. "Yes. It's so awful."

"What's going on?" Sasha asked.

"I can't tell you," Breeana replied.

"Why not? You can trust us," Jade insisted.

"If I told you, I could lose my sister forever," Breeana explained, "and I couldn't bear that. Cymbeline's the closest person in the world to me, and ever since we lost our mother..." Breeana broke down in tears again. Jade and Sasha hugged her until she calmed down enough to add, "I just wish my mum were here."

A magnolia blossom floated gently down towards the girls. Jade caught it and handed it to Breeana, making her smile.

"Can I ask what happened to your mum?" Jade asked softly.

Breeana looked down at the magnolia blossom in her hand, and then looked up at Jade and Sasha.

"Honestly, I don't know," she murmured. "No one does. It happened right before Cymbeline's birthday five years ago. Mum took us shopping. That's when she gave us our charm bracelets."

Breeana held up her wrist to show the girls a delicate bracelet with two pretty charms dangling from it.

"That's beautiful," Sasha said.

"Thank you," Breeana replied. "There used to be four charms — one for each member of our family. But now I guess it's just my dad and me..."

"You haven't really lost Cymbeline," Jade said, putting her arm around the younger girl. "She's just a little — confused right now, that's all."

"I hope you're right," Breeana whispered. She stared sadly at the two remaining charms on her bracelet, then shook herself out of it and continued. "It was a wonderful day. But then this freak blizzard hit town."

"Oh yeah, I remember that storm," Jade said. "It was the craziest thing."

"So what happened next?" Sasha asked.

"Well, I remember everything went dark, and my mum seemed scared," Breeana continued. "She hurried Cymbeline and me into a snow bank to keep us warm. Then I think she saw something, because she handed us her wand and told us it would protect us."

"She really had a wand?" Jade asked.

"Well — yeah," Breeana replied, flustered. "Um...I'll explain later."

"Of course," Sasha agreed. "Finish your story first."

"I'll always remember the last thing she said to us," Breeana murmured. "She said, 'Be brave, hold on to each other, never let go, and you'll be safe'." Tears trickled down her cheeks as she spoke. "Then the storm let up, but my mum was gone. And we never saw her again."

"I'm sorry," Jade said, her eyes wide. "I shouldn't have asked."

"It's really none of our business," Sasha added.

"No, it's okay," Breeana replied. "I've never talked about it before, but I actually feel better now that I've told someone."

"Well we're always happy to listen," Jade said, putting her arm around Breeana. "That's what friends are for, right?"

"Is there anything else, Breeana?" Sasha asked. "About what's going on with your sister?"

Breeana looked at her friends worriedly and sighed. "Okay, but you've gotta promise to keep this a secret."

"You can trust us," Jade insisted.

"I know, but...my dad has this thing about us not mixing too much with people from, you know, the outside..." Breeana told them.

"What do you mean, 'the outside'?" Sasha asked.

"Well...people who...aren't like us," Breeana continued. She looked from Jade to Sasha, and then slumped back against the tree hopelessly. They would never believe her. But then an idea struck her and she exclaimed, "Wait, I'll show you what I mean!"

63

Breeana led the girls into the mall and directly to a little shop they'd never really noticed before called 'Vivien's Secret'. She picked out two pairs of cute sunglasses, paid for them and then hurried the girls back outside.

"Okay, now put these on," Breeana said, handing the glasses to Jade and Sasha.

"But it's not even that sunny," Jade protested.

"Just try it," Breeana insisted. "But you can't tell anyone! My dad would banish me."

"Over a pair of sunglasses?" Sasha asked, putting hers on.

"Whoa," Jade exclaimed. With the glasses on, everything suddenly looked different – brighter, more colourful, and totally amazing! Jade and Sasha stood with their mouths open in complete disbelief.

"See, our world can choose when to reveal itself," Breeana explained. "But with these, you can choose."

Chapter 7

The girls headed back into the mall, where they saw that the shop they'd just come out of now featured a huge, sparkly sign reading 'Vivien's BIGGER Secret' – and it was now a fairy superstore! Fairy families strutted through the mall, looking hip and totally stylish, with wings sprouting from their backs.

A flock of pixies flew up to a miniature cashpoint, stuck in their cards and retrieved tiny gold coins, which they dropped into silky satchels before flying away.

Jade peered over her glasses at a normal-looking businessman sitting on a nearby bench. Then she looked at him through her sunglasses and saw that he had wings protruding from his suit jacket. He was reading a newspaper written in an elaborate, scrolling fairy-script.

"This is amazing!" Jade exclaimed.

"So why would your dad banish you for showing this to us?" Sasha asked.

"Well, he's the King of the fairies," Breeana explained. "He oversees all of nature and does lots of good things that we can't let ordinary people interfere with."

"Wow," Sasha exclaimed. "So you're, like, a fairy princess?"

Breeana nodded modestly.

"Wait, so is the Magnolia Ball one of his good works?" Jade asked.

"Yep," Breeana replied.

"So Yas and Cloe really did see Cymbeline sprout wings?" Sasha asked.

"Yeah, they did," Breeana admitted. "Fairies get their

©MGA

wings and magical powers when they turn eighteen. Cymbeline begged my dad to let her have hers early, but he refused."

"So how did Cymbeline get her wings?" Jade asked.

"I don't know," Breeana said. "But if my dad found out, he'd totally freak. All I know is, Cymbeline's been sneaking off somewhere at night, and I'm sure that has something to do with it."

"I wish we could follow her," Jade said. "But we can't exactly fly after her."

"Your friends can't fly, and they're going to the party with Cymbeline," Breeana pointed out. "So maybe we could follow them!"

"But the party's tonight," Sasha replied. "And so is the ball."

"We'll just have to miss the ball," Jade declared. "This is more important." She put her arm around Breeana, and the younger girl smiled gratefully at her friends.

At home Breeana crept into her kitchen and towards the sliding glass door. Then a voice behind her whispered, "Top o' the evening to you."

Breeana jumped with fright. She whirled around and saw her sister standing in the middle of the kitchen.

"Cymbeline!" she gasped.

Cymbeline stepped out of the shadows. She was all dressed up for a party. She looked her sister's outfit up and down, and asked disdainfully, "Is that what you're wearing?"

"What do you mean?" Breeana asked.

"Aren't you coming with me tonight?" Cymbeline continued.

"I didn't know you wanted me to," Breeana replied. "Besides, what about the Magnolia Ball?"

"Oh please," Cymbeline scoffed. "A loser charity ball? That's Dad's thing, not ours. My party's gonna be so much better — you can't miss it."

Breeana still looked reluctant, but Cymbeline continued, "Come on, I was going to tell you my secret tonight. And believe me, it's incredible."

Cymbeline put her arm around her sister, and Breeana gave in. "Okay. But let me put on something cuter first."

"Cool," Cymbeline replied. "Get ready to finally have some fun, little one."

Outside the front gate, Sasha and Jade sat in Sasha's convertible, waiting for Breeana.

"She's not coming," Jade announced. "I mean, it's already eight-thirty."

"Maybe we'd better go and find Cloe and Yasmin and follow them ourselves," Sasha suggested.

"They've probably already left," Jade sighed. "We missed our chance."

Sasha started the engine, but just as she was about to pull away, the gate swung open. Breeana darted out, glancing nervously over her shoulder as she made a mad dash for the car.

"Hurry!" Breeana cried as she hopped into the car. "I barely got away from my sister."

Sasha zoomed away from the Devlin house.

"We're worried that Cloe and Yasmin will have already left," Jade said.

Breeana craned her neck to look out of the window and saw a bright point of white light streaking across the sky.

"It's okay," Breeana replied. "I think I know where they're going. Head for the woods."

The girls parked beside the forest and crept through the dark woods towards Widow's Hollow.

"Are you sure about this?" Jade asked nervously.

"Widow's Hollow is where I saw Lina and her dark fairy friends capture Cloe and Yasmin," Breeana explained. "It's got to be some sort of home base for them."

The girls burst through the trees into Widow's Hollow. The lilies Dylan had tossed in the air lay crumpled on the ground, but otherwise the spot was totally deserted.

"Maybe I should've just gone with Cymbeline," Breeana said. "Then at least I could've found out what was going on."

"No way," Sasha replied. "Who knows what she had in mind for you?"

"Wait, what's that?" Jade asked. The three girls paused to listen to the sound of a pounding techno beat from somewhere in the distance.

"That's weird," Sasha said. "Where could that music be coming from?"

"I don't know," Breeana declared, "but we're gonna find out."

She led the other two deeper into the woods, towards the sound of the music. But as they walked, they noticed the sound of tiny feet scurrying after them.

The three girls stopped, and Jade whispered, "I think someone's following us." They looked around anxiously, but when they didn't hear anything else, Breeana insisted that they keep going.

The music got louder, and soon they saw eerie lights glowing between the trees. The girls hid in the undergrowth, looking up towards a hill with a large, withered tree growing on top of it. The music seemed to be coming from under the hill.

"What is this place?" Jade asked.

"It looks like a fairy mound," Breeana replied. "C'mon, let's check it out."

The three girls crept towards a crevice at the base of the hill.

"I think we can get in through here," Sasha said.

"Wait," Breeana whispered. She pulled a pouch out of her pocket. "Just let me sprinkle you guys with some of this first."

"Whoa," Jade said, backing away. "What is that?"

"It's fairy dust," Breeana explained. "It'll give you fairy sight, just like those glasses I bought you. If you can't see the fairy world like I can, Lina and her friends might be able to trick you."

"Okay," Jade agreed. Breeana sprinkled glittery dust over her friends, and suddenly the world seemed to come alive with huge, blooming wildflowers and tiny, twinkling lights.

"Wow," Sasha murmured.

"Let's go," Breeana urged.

©MGA

She pulled her mum's little purple wand out of her bag and held it out in front of her.

"What're you doing with that?" Jade asked.

"It'll protect us against dark fairies," Breeana said.

The girls crept towards the entrance to the fairy mound and slipped through the crevice that led under the hill. On the other side, they stepped onto an industrial-looking catwalk.

"Whoa..." Jade gasped, looking down at what seemed to be a huge, subterranean nightclub.

Chapter 8

Far below the girls, a wild-looking fairy DJ spun tunes as dark fairies with glow-in-the-dark wings and outfits danced to the music. Their moves were super-hip, but they were all dancing in a big circle around the dance floor. "What's going on here?" Jade asked.

"It's a fairy circle!" Breeana cried, with a note of panic in her voice.

"This music rocks!" Sasha exclaimed.

"I could dance to it forever!" Jade added.

"That's what I was afraid of," Breeana said. "I just can't believe it's a real fairy circle. My mum warned us about them – they're really bad, dark magic!"

"What's so bad about a fairy circle?" Jade scoffed. "It looks like fun."

"Yeah, too much fun," Breeana replied. "If you ever join one, you become entranced, and you end up a servant of the dark fairies."

"Forever?" Sasha asked.

"Forever," Breeana told her. "Or until you find a way to break the spell."

The girls spotted Cymbeline dancing in the centre of the crowd. Lina danced beside her, a gleeful smirk plastered across her face.

"There's Cymbeline!" Jade exclaimed.

"She's under a spell too," Breeana said. "I'm sure of it. And I have to save her."

"We'll help you," Jade declared.

"No," Breeana insisted. "You have to get out of here. Your friends are already enchanted because they tried to help my sister and me. And I've put you two in enough danger already."

"We're not leaving," Sasha replied.

"Yeah! Friends stick together," Jade added.

"And we're not gonna let you down," Sasha finished.

Breeana looked torn, but when she saw how determined Jade and Sasha were, she smiled and took their hands. "Thanks, you guys." With a deep breath, she said, "Okay, let's go. And whatever you do – no dancing!"

"No dancing?" Sasha groaned as she reluctantly pulled herself away. "But these are totally hot tunes. This won't be easy!"

The girls hugged the walls, staying just outside the fairy circle. Everyone was so caught up in their dancing that no one seemed to notice them. They had almost reached the other side of the dance floor when Lina called over the loudspeaker, "Stop the music! I have an announcement!"

The music stopped, and everyone turned to look at Lina. Breeana, Sasha and Jade hid in the shadows, praying they wouldn't be spotted.

"Soon I'll have finished the job I started five

whole years ago!" she declared. "Where's the Princess?"

The crowd of dark fairies jeered as Cymbeline stepped onto the catwalk beside Lina.

"I thought Cymbeline here would be hard work," Lina explained, "but she was so eager to get her wings early – and I, well, I was more than happy to help her. Before long, she was breaking the rules at home – and with them, the heart of her stinking royal family!"

The crowd of fairies cheered and clapped as Lina continued. "Thank heavens for rebellious teens! As each of the King's family members falls, those who remain grow weaker, and I grow stronger!"

Breeana glanced down worriedly at the two remaining charms on her bracelet.

"Soon I'll have Breeana too," Lina announced, "and then the great Fairy King himself will be at my mercy!"

The dark fairies cheered wildly.

"Lina must be the 'evil one' I've heard my dad talk about." Breeana gasped.

"Fairies have served the earth long enough," Lina shouted. "But once I'm in control, the earth is gonna serve us!"

She motioned to the DJ to start up the music, and soon the party was hopping again.

"What do we do now?" Jade asked.

"I-I-" Breeana began weakly. She looked like she was about to faint, and the girls stepped forward to prop her up.

"Breeana, what's wrong?" Sasha asked.

"I feel...funny..." Breeana murmured. She slumped into her friends' arms.

"That's it, we're getting you out of here," Sasha announced. They started to guide Breeana back the way they'd come, but Breeana resisted.

"No!" she cried. "I have to help my sister."

"We'll have to find some other way to help her," Jade declared. She and Sasha dragged Breeana towards the door, but Cloe and Yasmin appeared in their path, stopping them. The girls swayed to the pounding music as though hypnotized, totally blending in with the crowd in their glow-in-the-dark fairy fashions. Yasmin danced right up to Sasha but didn't really seem to see her.

"Yas! Look at me!" Sasha exclaimed, waving her hands in front of Yasmin's face. "Snap out of it!"

"Snap outta what?" Yasmin demanded impatiently.

Sasha turned to Jade and Breeana hopelessly.

"Wait!" Breeana said. "I know what we can do. We have to hold hands and make a circle around them."

"What?" Jade asked. "Why?"

©MGA

"Quick!" Breeana insisted. "Just do it."

Sasha, Jade and Breeana joined hands in a circle around Cloe and Yasmin.

"It's a counter-spell my mum taught me," Breeana explained.

"Hey, what are you doing?" Cloe cried. "Aren't you girls a little old for ring around the roses? Geez, Sasha, I'm so sick of you acting like such a child."

"Angel! How can you say that?" Sasha gasped.

"Easy," Yasmin replied. "She's never really liked you. Face it, Sasha — you've never been cool enough to hang with us."

Sasha and Jade exchanged horrified looks.

"Breeana, I don't think this circle thing is working," Jade whispered.

"It will," Breeana promised. "Be brave. Just remember, your friends are in there somewhere. It's not really them saying these things — it's the enchantment."

"Don't listen to her, Kool Kat," Cloe

interrupted. "She's just a freshman – what does she know?"

"Angel! You called me Kool Kat!" Jade exclaimed, relieved.

"Of course I did," Cloe cooed, suddenly sweet. "You're my best friend forever! Come on, let's lose these freaky people." She reached for Jade's hand. "Get me outta here, Kool Kat!"

Jade took Cloe's hand, breaking the circle.

"No, Jade!" Breeana yelled, but it was too late. She slumped into Sasha's arms, weakened by the dark magic all around her.

"Ha ha," Cloe said with a smirk. She yanked her hand away from Jade's and declared, "April Fool's has come and passed, and you're the biggest fools at last!"

"Why are you talking like that?" Sasha

asked.

Without answering, Cloe and Yasmin whirled and snatched Breeana away from Sasha.

"Stop it!" Sasha cried. "Let her go!"

"Run!" Breeana whispered. "Get out of here before they enchant you too."

Dylan appeared beside the girls and grabbed Jade's arm, pulling her towards the fairy circle. "Fancy a dance?" he enquired.

Jade wriggled out of Dylan's grasp.

"Sorry, Dylan. I can't dance right now."

She tried to help Sasha pull Breeana away from Cloe and Yasmin, putting the younger girl in the middle of a tug of war.

"Join the dance!" Yasmin cried.

"The fun never ends!" Cloe added.

"Let her go!" Jade shouted.

The music stopped suddenly and Lina strolled

over to the girls with an evil grin on her face. "I knew you'd show up, Breeana. So glad you could come to my party."

Yasmin and Cloe led Breeana over to Lina while Dylan and a group of dark fairies pushed Sasha and Jade away.

"Wouldn't you like some wings like your sister's?" Lina asked. "Why wait? I mean, having to do good deeds to sprout the wings you're entitled to? Who needs it?" Breeana stared up at Lina weakly. "All you have to do is ask, and you can have your wings right now!" Lina declared.

She flicked her finger at Breeana and a shower of crimson sparks burst toward the girl's face. Breeana flinched as Jade and Sasha struggled to reach her. The dark fairies giggled cruelly as they held them back.

"Come on, Breeana," Cymbeline said. "It's so wonderful! Just think, you and I can fly away together!"

"Don't do it, Breeana!" Sasha pleaded. "It's not worth it!"

"Take my hand, Breeana," Lina commanded. "Come fly with me." Breeana bit her lower lip, looking uncertain. She slowly reached her hand towards Lina's. The entire room fell silent as everyone waited to see what Breeana would do.

One of the two remaining charms on Breeana's bracelet trembled, about to fall off, and Lina smiled. "That's it," she said encouragingly. But then Breeana pulled out her mum's wand and flung a handful of fairy dust into Lina's face.

"Aaahhhh!" Lina shrieked, cringing. "I can't see!"

The dark fairies all cringed too, as though they felt the same pain Lina did.

A fierce wind whipped through the club as the dark fairies moaned, "Aaaaahhhh!"

Holding her wand out, Breeana shoved Cloe and Yasmin out of the way and darted towards Sasha and Jade.

"Run!" she shouted.

The three girls dashed into a nearby tunnel. Lina blinked the fairy dust out of her eyes just in time to see Breeana making her escape.

"You know what?" Lina said. "This club is totally tired. Time to hit the next party!"

She threw her hand into the air and a bright crimson flash flew from her fingertips. With a bang, all the lights went out. The fairies' neon outfits glowed in the darkness as they streamed out of the cavern.

Breeana, Sasha and Jade were running through the tunnel when suddenly everything went black. They heard a loud rumbling and crashing sound all around them. Jade and Sasha screamed — just before everything went completely silent.

Chapter 9

Back at the magnolia tree, the Magnolia Ball was well underway. A DJ spun tunes as a crowd of people, all dressed up, danced under the sweeping branches of the magnolia tree.

"I apologize for my girls, Mayor Davis," Mel Devlin was saying to a middle-aged woman. "It's not like them to be so late."

"I know you wanted them to be here, but I don't think we should wait any longer to get started," the Mayor replied. "I'm sure they'll turn up soon."

Mel looked anxious, but the Mayor continued, "Cymbeline's done such a wonderful job of leading this committee — I'm sure she wouldn't miss the whole event! She's probably just handling some last-minute details." Mayor Davis patted Mel's hand reassuringly. "You must be so proud of her."

"I am," Mel agreed softly.

"Well, we're up," the Mayor said, leading Mel towards a small stage set up beneath the tree. She strode up to the microphone and the DJ cut the music.

"Citizens of Stilesville," she began, "as your mayor, I want to sincerely thank all of you for making our annual Magnolia Ball such a success! As you know, this event was inspired by this beautiful magnolia tree, which was planted here anonymously five years ago."

The crowd murmured appreciatively as they gazed up at the tree, lit majestically against the night sky.

"In honour of this gorgeous Stilesville landmark, all proceeds from tonight's event will benefit ecological renewal throughout the county."

The crowd applauded as the Mayor gestured for Mel to join her.

"And now, it's my great honour to introduce

the Magnolia Ball's generous sponsor, Mr Mel Devlin!"

Loud applause greeted Mel as he stepped timidly up to the podium.

"Good evening. I, uh, I..." Mel's voice trailed off as he noticed the dark clouds rolling in and heard the eerie beat of the dark fairies' music in the distance.

A cluster of neon lights appeared in the sky and a frightened murmur arose from the crowd. Moments later, the dark fairies landed, swarming through the party and pushing the townspeople aside. Cloe, Yasmin and Dylan were deposited under the tree by three dark fairies they'd ridden in with.

The dark fairy DJ landed on the stage and knocked the other DJ aside. He blasted his techno tunes and the crowd started swaying to the beat, blank smiles spreading across their faces. The dark fairies formed a circle around the crowd and joined the dance.

Lina landed next to Mel and exclaimed, "Hey there, Mel!"

"Lina?" Mel asked, shocked. "I banished you for all eternity!"

"Yeah, well, I escaped," Lina replied with a shrug. She winked at Mel and added, "Can't keep a bad girl down, ya know." She looked Mel up and down and grimaced. "Ick – lose the dorky disguise already. The civilians are all enchanted anyway."

She waved a hand at Mel and a crimson ripple washed over him. His average, middle-aged-dad look evaporated, revealing him as King Melvino, a commanding, muscular man with flowing hair and a pair of golden wings.

"Well, they aren't going to stay enchanted," he declared in a booming voice. He raised his hand majestically and said, "I banish you to–"

But Lina interrupted him with her scornful laughter. "I don't think so," she snapped. "Oh, Cymbeline! Come show Daddy what Auntie Lina gave you."

King Melvino's forehead creased with worry as he watched his daughter stride towards him. "Cymbeline?" he asked. "What's going on here?"

Cymbeline smirked at her father as wings burst out of her back in a shower of light. She shook them out saucily and crossed her arms over her chest, daring her father to say anything to her.

Instead, he turned on Lina. "Wings? You gave her wings?!"

"Every fairy wants her wings," Lina replied with a laugh.

"But she–" King Melvino protested.

"She has deserted you to join me," Lina interrupted him. "Which, of course, weakens your power. Oh, and I wouldn't expect Breeana to surface any time soon, either."

King Melvino stared at his nemesis in horror. "What have you done to Breeana?" he demanded.

"I had to get rid of her," Lina replied offhandedly.

Back in the tunnel, Jade flipped open her mobile phone and used the light from the screen to track down her friends.

"Sasha? Breeana?" she called. She heard the other girls coughing near the floor of the tunnel and followed the sound to them. In the blue glow of her mobile phone, Jade saw that boulders and a tree trunk had collapsed into the tunnel around them, and twisted pieces of metal poked out of the rubble.

"Is everyone okay?" Sasha asked, dusting herself off.

"What happened?" Jade looked around, stunned, at all the wreckage.

"I think Lina collapsed the mound on us," Breeana explained. She tried climbing up a pile of rocks that sloped up towards the ceiling, but they slid away under her feet and she had to scramble to keep from falling.

"We're completely blocked in," Jade declared. "We'll never climb or dig our way out of here."

Sasha looked at her phone and sighed. "No signal."

"What're we gonna do?" Jade asked, her voice rising in panic.

"I don't know, Kool Kat," Sasha

©MGA

replied. "Our friends are all under a spell and my phone doesn't work and – well, I think we're really trapped."

The girls looked at each other worriedly. They were starting to give up hope when they heard a small scratching sound above them.

"Listen," Breeana whispered. "It's getting closer."

"What is that?" Jade asked.

"I don't know," Sasha said.

Suddenly, a bunch of rocks tumbled down towards them, and a thin, yellow shaft of moonlight pierced the darkness. More rocks fell inward, and a hole appeared at the top of the cavern. Then the scuffling sounds stopped and a tiny head appeared in the hole, silhouetted against the moon.

"Hellooo!" called an Irish voice. "Is that you girls I hear down there? Can you hear me? Are you there?"

"Alfie?" Breeana asked. "I think it's our gnome!" she whispered to her friends.

Alfie held a lantern out in front of him, revealing his face and filling the cavern with light.

"And who were you expecting?" Alfie enquired. "Me cousin Barry the Leprechaun, perhaps? Well, I hate to disappoint you, but it's just me here. Now, stand back and I'll have the three of you out of there quicker than you can say 'Tipperary'!"

The girls backed away from the hole and watched as Alfie chipped away at the rocks with a little pick. He disappeared for a moment and, when he returned, he sent a flurry of tiny sprites down into the cavern. The sprites flitted around Sasha, Jade and Breeana, grabbing on to them and lifting them up through the opening in the ceiling of the tunnel. Jade and Sasha looked around in amazement as they floated out of the cavern.

The sprites set them down outside the collapsed mound and then flew off into the night.

Alfie leaned on his pick and held his lantern out towards the girls.

"That looks like that creepy garden gnome we saw by the magnolia tree," Sasha whispered. Jade nodded slowly.

Alfie marched up to Sasha and snapped, "Creepy, am I? Well, I'll be remindin' you 'tis a creepy garden gnome who's responsible for you bein' up here in the world instead of trapped in that hole."

Sasha backed away, waving her hands in front of her apologetically. "Hey, sorry, dude. Really, I didn't—"

"Alfie's me name, and don't you forget it!" the gnome interrupted. "I'm the guardian of the Devlin clan, so I am." Then he called over his shoulder, "I think it's fair to say the girls are safe now!"

"Yahoo!" cheered an army of gnomes, stepping forward from the shadows.

"Wow," Jade murmured. "It's, like, a gnome nation."

"Alfie, you saved our lives!" Breeana exclaimed, swooping the little man up in a hug.

Alfie blushed as he replied, "We little people will never let the dark fairies have their way, no we won't!"

"Lousy dark fairies!" grumbled the crowd of gnomes.

"But where did the dark fairies go?" Breeana asked, setting Alfie down again. "And where did they take Cloe and Yasmin and Dylan?"

"Your friends were carried away," Alfie explained. "Off to another party, I heard them say."

"I bet they went to the ball!" Jade cried.

"They're after my father!" Breeana gasped. "We'll never get there in time."

She was interrupted by a loud whinny. A winged unicorn pranced forward, tossing her head.

"Dempsey!" Breeana exclaimed.

"Did ye think I wouldn't be bringin' transportation?" Alfie asked.

Breeana hopped onto Dempsey's back.

"Is there room for two more?" Sasha asked.

Before Alfie could answer, two more winged unicorns stepped out of the shadows.

"Wha – what do we...?" Jade stammered.

"You just jump onto the animal and off you go like the wind." Alfie shook his head in frustration. "Oh, you are such a pair of silly billies! I don't know why I even bother."

The girls looked at each other and shrugged, then climbed onto the unicorns' backs. Groups of gnomes jumped on after them. The three unicorns leapt into the air, soaring across the night sky.

"Off we go!" shouted the gnomes.

"Go, Dempsey!" Breeana cheered.

Sasha and Jade clung tightly to their unicorns' manes, but when they saw how calm Breeana looked, they relaxed and took in the breathtaking view of the entire town of Stilesville twinkling below them. In the distance, a dark cluster of clouds hung low over the town square.

"That's where the ball is!" Jade exclaimed, pointing.

Alfie popped his head out of Dempsey's saddlebag.

"Can't you go any faster, you mule?" he demanded.

Dempsey whinnied and beat her wings harder.

Chapter 10

Beneath the magnolia tree, Lina and King Melvino circled each other, their eyes burning with fury. "What do you want, Queen of Mischief?" he growled.

"Girls just wanna have fun–" she began playfully, but Melvino stopped her.

"Speak plainly!" he shouted.

"Fine," Lina hissed. "I want you out of the way. And I want the fairy kingdom to be all mine!"

"Never!" King Melvino declared.

"Oh, don't be boring," Lina sighed. "You can't stand in my way, any more than your wife could."

"My wife?" King Melvino asked, narrowing his eyes suspiciously.

"Um, hello? Freak blizzard five years ago? You didn't really think that came out of nowhere, did you?" Lina laughed in Melvino's face, making him wince.

"You..." he sneered.

"That's right," Lina replied. "You know, your wife figured out right away that it was my doing. And she knew it wasn't gonna be pretty." She shook her finger at King Melvino. "Of course, this all could've been avoided if only you hadn't banished me. Really, you have only yourself to blame."

"What did you do to her?" Melvino demanded.

"There was an incredible battle of spells," Lina explained. "I must say, your Dee was a fierce opponent. But ultimately, I won out, as I knew I would. Too bad it took me five years to rebuild my strength, but — ta-da! I'm back! And thanks to your daughters, I'm now stronger than even you."

"We'll see about that," King Melvino held his arm out towards his daughter and cried, "Cymbeline!" A flash of golden light washed over her and the rest of the crowd. Slowly, the guests began to come to, blinking in confusion.

"Wh-what happened?" Cloe asked.

"What's going on?" Dylan added.

Cymbeline's wings disappeared and she shook her head to clear it.

"Daddy!" she exclaimed, running over to her father. "I'm so sorry!"

King Melvino put his arm around her comfortingly.

"And now for you!" he shouted at Lina. He flung his hand towards her, but she countered with a flash of crimson light. Their spells collided in mid-air, and hers began to push his back. King Melvino resisted with all his strength, but Lina's spell overpowered his, forcing him backwards. He staggered under the blast of her magic.

"Ha! You wasted too much energy saving those measly townspeople," Lina taunted him. She waved her hand and King Melvino flew off the stage, landing hard in the dirt.

"Ugh!" he gasped.

Cymbeline rushed to her father's side.

"No!" Cymbeline cried.

Lina waved her hand again, and Cymbeline flew through the air. She crashed against the magnolia tree and crumpled to the ground, unconscious.

"Oh no!" Cloe exclaimed. She and Yasmin hurried to Cymbeline's side, while Lina strode over to King Melvino.

"You foul, conniving witch," he hissed, staggering to his feet.

"Yep, that's me," Lina agreed. "Now say bye-bye..." she raised her arms and began casting a spell, "...cos now it's time to join your wife."

A fierce wind whipped around King Melvino. Then a bolt of lightning struck him as thunder ripped through the air. The townspeople tried to rush forward to help him, but the dark fairies held them back. Lina cackled in triumph but, just as quickly, her powers began to diminish.

"What's going on?" she demanded. "This spell should be a breeze."

A mighty whinny burst through the air. Lina jerked her head towards the sky and saw Breeana, Jade and Sasha swooping down at her on their flying unicorns.

"How did they escape?" Lina demanded. She turned to the other dark fairies and commanded, "Stop them! Keep them away from me!"

Breeana landed beside her, and Lina dropped to her knees, the power seeping out of her. Still, she kept shooting firebolts at Mel, who doubled over in pain.

Jade and Sasha skidded to a stop in front of

the crowd, and their gnome friends spilled out onto the dance floor. A dark fairy tried to grab Sasha, but her unicorn head-butted the fairy, knocking her down. "Thanks!" Sasha cried, hugging her unicorn's neck.

Breeana, Jade and Sasha pushed through the crowd, trying to reach Lina. But the dark fairies stood in a tight circle around their leader, protecting her so she could finish her spell.

Out of the crowd, they heard a familiar voice call, "Bunny Boo, Kool Kat, help us!"

They turned and saw Yasmin and Cloe crouching beside Cymbeline. Breeana, Jade and Sasha rushed over to join them. Breeana fell to the ground beside her sister, but the other two hung back for a moment, looking suspiciously at their friends.

"Hey Cloe, I heard you failed your chemistry class," Sasha said.

"What? Omigosh, I'm totally ruined!" Cloe cried.

105

"I think they're back to normal," Jade told Sasha. They rushed forward to hug their best friends, relieved to have them back at last.

"Cymbeline, wake up!" Breeana begged, shaking her sister. "Please wake up!"

Breeana glanced towards her father and saw that he was being stretched and contorted under the strain of Lina's spell.

"Must...finish — must... succeed!" Lina shouted.

"You've got to

©MGA

stop her!" Sasha told Breeana.

"As soon as she finishes with your dad, she'll turn on you," Jade added. "You're the only one who can save him."

"But I'm powerless!" Breeana cried, tears streaming down her face.

"Can't we try another fairy circle?" Jade said. "I promise I'll hold on this time."

Breeana looked uncertain. "I don't think I can do it without my sister," she said.

As she spoke, a gentle breeze rustled through the blossoms of the magnolia tree. A single petal floated down and landed on Cymbeline's forehead. A warm, white glow spread across her face, and her cheeks flushed with colour. Her eyes fluttered, then opened. She looked up at the branches above her and whispered, "Mum?"

The girls all turned to Cymbeline, thrilled to see her awake. But before they could celebrate, they heard a long, sorrowful moan, and whirled to see King Melvino being transformed into a mighty tree.

"A tree!" Breeana gasped, looking from her father to the magnolia tree. "This — this tree — it's my mum!"

"Lina turned her into a tree?!" Sasha cried.

"It's a powerful spell, but there is a counter-spell," Breeana replied. "Remember, Cymbeline? She showed it to us once, when we were little."

Breeana climbed to her feet, then helped her sister up. "I remember," Cymbeline whispered.

"Remember what she said to us, the last time we saw her?" Breeana asked.

"Be brave..." Cymbeline began.

"... hold on to each other..." Breeana continued.

"Never let go, and you'll be safe," Cymbeline finished.

The sisters shared a determined look, and then reached for their friends' hands.

Chapter 11

Yasmin, Cloe, Jade and Sasha joined hands with Cymbeline and Breeana, forming a fairy circle around the base of the magnolia tree. As they completed their circle, a white light shot up the tree's trunk, reaching all the way to its farthest branches.

Lina felt the surge of energy and turned towards the girls, but she was too busy struggling to finish her spell on King Melvino to interfere.

"Stop them!" she ordered her minions.

The dark fairies swarmed towards the circle of girls, but the flying unicorns and the army of gnomes leapt forward to intercept them.

"Yaaahhh!" Alfie cried, charging forward. A dark fairy guy ran towards him, hands raised to cast a spell. Alfie grabbed two tarts from a nearby dessert table and smashed them into the dark fairy's eyes. The fairy staggered, green sparks flying from his fingertips as he continued to cast his spell. Alfie ducked and the spell hit a dark fairy girl, who fell to the ground. Alfie grabbed a chocolate cake and slipped it onto the ground – just before the fairy fell face-first into it, splattering icing everywhere. Then Alfie grabbed a cookie

©MGA

and chomped on it as he darted forward to keep fighting.

Cymbeline, Breeana and their friends ignored the commotion, focusing on the tree, which glowed serenely.

Lina glanced over at them worriedly.

"Give it up, girls!" she shouted. "You'll never survive the counter-spell!"

As the girls focused on the tree, it turned into a giant, blue-white column of ice. The girls shivered in the unbearable cold, their breath puffing in front of them.

"Be brave... hold on to each other..." Breeana murmured.

"I can't take it!" Cymbeline cried.

Then the tree burst into flames that licked at the sky. The girls shrieked.

"Be brave!" Breeana insisted. "Hold on to each other!"

"Never let go!" Cymbeline added, bracing herself.

The tree turned into a writhing mass of snakes. The snakes hissed in the girls' faces, flicking their tongues and baring their fangs. The girls cringed and nearly broke away, but they all chanted together, "Be brave... hold on to each other...never let go."

The tree began to tremble, and the girls looked on in terror. They were about to flee when a huge rumble burst from the roots, and the snakes were sucked back into the tree. Then a blinding white light burst out of the tree, enveloping the girls in its brilliant glow.

Everyone at the party froze, stunned by the beautiful, bright light. Then the light was absorbed inwards, leaving the slender, lovely Dee Devlin standing in the middle of the circle. She gazed proudly at her daughters and their friends.

"Well done, girls," she said.

Then she whirled and flung a spell at the dark fairies. They all vanished with an eerie shriek.

But Lina had already finished casting her spell on Melvino. She collapsed to the ground, exhausted.

"You're too late, Dee," she hissed. "My spell is complete."

"Yeah, but here's the thing," Breeana replied. "Now we know how to break it."

"Hmm, that does present a problem," Lina admitted.

"Take my hands, girls," Dee told her daughters. Breeana and Cymbeline each took one of her hands. Jade noticed that each of them had four charms dangling from her bracelet again.

"Together, we're more than a match for them," Dee declared.

She raised her hands, clasped in her daughters', and a wave of white energy surged across the square, knocking Lina to the ground.

"Uhhh," Lina moaned.

The new tree blew apart in a burst of white energy, leaving King Melvino standing in its place.

"Darling!" he exclaimed, rushing to embrace his wife.

"Melvino," Dee murmured.

They pulled their daughters into a hug. Then Melvino turned to Lina, who was dusting herself off and climbing to her feet.

"As for you — no need for that dorky disguise," he told her.

He waved his hand, and a golden ripple washed over Lina. She turned into a raven.

"Selfishness doesn't look so good, after all," he declared.

"Are you gonna banish me again?" the raven squawked.

"Yes," King Melvino replied. "And the next time you challenge a king, remember this: a spell that takes you five years to perfect, takes me but a minute."

With that, he zapped Lina into a withered, scrawny tree.

"Amateur," he scoffed. He turned back to his family, and they all hugged again.

Chapter 12

"Thank goodness you're all safe," Melvino cried, holding his wife and daughters close.

"Dad, I'm so sorry," Cymbeline whispered. "This is all my fault. I broke the rules—"

"Shh, it's all right," her father murmured, stroking her hair. "It's all over now."

"I broke the rules too," Breeana admitted. "I gave Sasha and Jade fairy sight."

Her father's eyes narrowed. "You what?" he demanded, frowning.

"Dad, she did it for me," Cymbeline protested.

"Without my friends, I could never have stopped Lina!" Breeana explained.

Melvino stared at his daughter and she peered up at him, frightened. But then a calm smile spread across his face.

"I know that your motive was love, not selfishness," he declared. "Your instincts saved us all. And you know, maybe it wouldn't hurt if I lightened up a little on the rules about non-fairy folk."

He turned to Jade, Cloe, Sasha and Yasmin and announced, "As for you, my family owes you a debt of gratitude."

"We're just glad we could help, sir," Jade replied.

"It takes great

©MGA

bravery to survive the counter-spell to a dark fairy's enchantment," Dee told the girls.

Dee exchanged a look with her husband, and he nodded approvingly. She raised her hand and a shimmering glow swept over her daughters. Glittering wings burst forth from their backs.

"Our wings!" Breeana exclaimed.

"Mum, are you sure?" Cymbeline asked.

"I'm sure," her mother replied. "You've earned them." She turned to Jade, Cloe, Sasha and Yasmin and added, "And you ladies have earned the right to keep your knowledge of the Fairy Kingdom."

"But I'm afraid that you can never tell anyone else," King Melvino added. "And unfortunately, I must remove your fairy sight forever."

"How'd I know he was gonna say that?" Sasha sighed.

Melvino passed his hand over the girls' eyes, and they blinked. Everything looked normal again —

Melvino looked like ordinary old Mel, and everyone's wings had disappeared.

"If you ever need fairy godparents, you know where we are," Dee told them.

"Sounds good to me," Cloe replied.

Mel raised his hand and a golden light swept over Dylan and the rest of the guests.

"It's a spell of forgetfulness," he explained.

The DJ turned on the music and the guests started dancing again as if nothing had happened.

"Oh no!" cried a plump lady, noticing the withered Lina-tree. "What happened to our magnolia tree? It's all shrivelled and ugly!"

"I'll dig it up tomorrow and plant a new one," the Mayor promised.

Mel and Dee shared a smile, and Mel held a hand out to his wife.

"Shall we dance, darling?" he asked.

Dee took her husband's hand, and they floated

onto the dance floor as their daughters looked on happily.

Dylan hobbled up to his friends and moaned, "My thighs are killing me! It's like I've been strapped on a vicious dance machine for days!" He noticed Breeana standing nearby and shot her a grin. "But that doesn't mean I don't have one dance left for you, little lady."

"Me?" Breeana gasped excitedly. "You're asking me to dance?"

"Is it safe to dance now?" Sasha asked Breeana.

"Yes, it's definitely safe to dance now," Breeana replied, taking Dylan's outstretched hand.

"So," Cloe began, turning to Sasha and Jade. "Why are Yas and I wearing these wings? And what, exactly, happened here? I have a strange feeling we've missed a lot."

"Cloe, this time your strange feeling is right

on," Jade replied.

"We'll explain everything," Sasha promised.

As the four best friends walked away, Jade said to Sasha, "Do you think we'll believe it in the morning? Or will it all seem like a dream?"

"Oh, I have a feeling we'll believe it," Sasha said with a grin. She pulled the sunglasses Breeana had given her out of her bag and put them on, giggling. Then she tripped and fell.

"Argh! Who put this creepy garden gnome here?" Alfie glared up at her and she added, "Oh – sorry Alfie – I take it back, I swear!"

Cloe, Jade and Yasmin giggled as Sasha tried to soothe the glowering gnome.

"Come on, Sasha, let's go home," Jade said, slinging her arm around Sasha's shoulders. "I think you've had enough excitement for one day."

"I think I just might've had enough excitement for one lifetime," Sasha declared.

"Aw, you're just sayin' that," Cloe teased. "You know you live for excitement."

As the girls laughed, Jade said, "I missed you guys."

"We missed you too," Yasmin replied.

©MGA

"Friends forever?" Sasha asked.

"Obviously!" Cloe said.

The girls linked arms and headed back to Cloe's place, relieved to be a foursome again.

Read more about the Bratz in
these other awesome books!

Spring Break Safari
Pet Project
Diamond Road Trip